Tourist at a Miracle

Other Books by Mark Statman

Listener in the Snow: The Practice and Teaching of Poetry

The Alphabet of the Trees: A Guide to Nature Writing (with Christian McEwen)

Poet in New York (Federico García Lorca, translated with Pablo Medina)

Tourist at a Miracle

Mark Statman

Hanging Loose Press
Brooklyn, New York

Published by Hanging Loose Press, 231 Wyckoff Street, Brooklyn, New York 11217.

www.hangingloosepress.com

Printed in the United States of America
10 9 8 7 6 5 4 3 2 1

Hanging Loose Press thanks the Literature Program of New York State Council on the Arts for a grant in support of the publication of this book.

Cover art by Katherine Koch
Cover design by Marie Carter

Library of Congress Cataloging-in-Publication Data

Statman, Mark
Tourist at a miracle / Mark Statman.
p. cm.
ISBN 978-1-934909-16-4 (pbk.)
I. Title.
PS3619.T3825T68 2010
811'.6--dc22

2009036335

for Katherine and Jesse

Contents

I. Conspiracy

Conspiracy 11
Kenneth's Death 13
Losing Buttons 14
The Call of God 15
How Nice This Is 16
My Own Hand 17
"Some kids" 18
The Evolution of Complexity 19
My Son 20
(A)political Poem 21
One Person 22
Late Afternoon 23
You and Me 24
Translating García Lorca 25
Invisible Man 26

II. Yellow

Please Read This 31
Turbulence 32
Changing 34
"A way to redeem the world" 36
A Love Affair with Perception 38
Poem Written in Silence 40
"You're in love" 41
A Hundred 42
A Word Gone Wrong 43
"Snow and ice" 44
Meditation 45
The Happy Problem 46

Blindness 48
The Bad Screenwriter 49
People Shouting 51
A Poem about Something Ending Is an Elegy 52
Subway Manners 53
Snow, Late March, in Brooklyn 55
Love in the Time of Cholera 56

III. Tourist at a Miracle

Tourist 61
More the Imagined than the Real 62
Fields 64
This Belongs To 65
Tubing 66
Fly Fishing 67
Late Night 68
Tú Quieres Saber 70
The Poetry City Hall of Fame 72
A Thousand Words 73
Neutral Location 75
Because I Live in This City 77
She Wanted to Be Looked At 78
Music Central 80
WTC (July 2006) 81
City Summers 83
Travel 85

I. Conspiracy

Conspiracy

for Katherine

there's that Ray Charles song
I can't stop loving you
it's not from my past
but a past beyond my past
so it's part of me
but only as memory
of a memory
I can't stop loving you
all choral
the first line
and then
the solo
I've made up my mind
it echoes
this is real
echo
redolent of spring and warmth
and those yellow and green days
before I was conscious
that loving you or anyone
meant anything

when I was young
those days
seemed unimportant and forever
and now they seem
too fast and everything
this walk in the dark
while you're away
reminds me

that I can't (stop)
I don't want to
past and memory suddenly present
conspiring into the future
I've made up my mind
wanting the mind
to have that much to do
with love

Kenneth's Death

he's dead and
I still don't believe:
years later
I'm walking someplace
and I'll think
this is something
I'll tell him
when he gets back
when he gets back
as though where Kenneth's gone
is simply too far away
to telephone or
send a postcard
which is why we haven't heard
for so long
from a man who couldn't stand
not to be in touch

when he gets back
we'll be up
half the night
a good bottle of wine
recommended by Sharon
at the liquor store
maybe even one of those
Cuban cigars he'd
stopped smoking
we'll be up half the night
and Kenneth won't
get in
a word

Losing Buttons

if I had a different
sense of things I'd write
with different words

it would still
be about avoiding
which is what I write about
but different words
would add another layer
to the unknown
and unacknowledged

there must be a museum
full of this:
a museum of falling away

I put stones on the graves
of people I don't know
but on the graves
of my family none

I have a stone left
flat and black
so I engrave my initials
on it, put it
in my pocket
then change my mind
and throw it into the river

in the dark
the letters glow
like ghosts

The Call of God

I wonder what that
would be like to hear
I wonder how it comes

Do you have to be
someplace specific
Walking on a road
Standing alone in the deep woods
Could it happen in a city,
in between the buildings
or on a street corner
with all the other people
moving around you

Even more
how do you recognize *it*
There are so many voices
in my head right now—
mine, Katherine's, Jesse's
the list here could continue
like going through a phone book
Maybe I've been hearing The Call all along
and I haven't known
which I guess is the difference
between The Voice and The Call.

The Voice just there,
The Call particularly
wanting you

Except why wouldn't God
want all of us

How Nice This Is

blue jays in the yard
scare other birds away
then come squirrels
and the jays retreat
cawing in the clouds

the day goes like that
arrivals, departures
I go to the couch
and think how nice this is
how it's how life should be
looking ahead I think
the whole house needs cleaning
all the walls need painting
I decide instead
to get outside

it's cold
which is good
breathing deeply
my eyes catch the eyes
of a small girl walking by
with her mother
she looks at me
eyes and eyes
she looks at me and smiles

My Own Hand

in some places
the streets are on a grid
but even that
predictability feels unreliable
in other places
it's all labyrinthine
and I keep passing
the same corner
with the same newspaper vendor
who the third or fourth time
smiles at me
and I try to convince myself
that I'm not looking
for a place, an address
I'm not lost
I'm wandering
but the wanderer is no more real
than the figures I imagine
in the clouds
or the sounds I imagine
I hear with my eyes closed
at the beach
after a while
the wind is only the wind
and those aren't voices
no matter how much
you want them to be
sometimes the only hand
I can take
is my own

Some kids

have started
a lemonade stand
(twenty-five cents a cup)
next to a building site

sounds of construction
jackhammers, yelling
a car honks
another joins in
and soon the dissonance
of car horns and construction
becomes all there is
in the hot and noisy air

I think how
I want to go someplace
where I don't have to think
about going someplace

I ask for another lemonade
ask one of the boys to put
an ice cube in
it will cost an extra nickel
he says
and I laugh
I tell him it's worth it
to have the ice on my tongue

The Evolution of Complexity

for Alan MacGowan

Why we love
is the first question

If there's a second one
I think this day
is too beautiful to ask it

The trees are blossoming
the air just smells *good*
despite the city, the world and
its newspaper news

I'm not really interested
in answers
I just like the question
Why we love
which invites the
inevitable response
How could we not

Okay, there's the second question

impossible to resist
on a day like today
and so many people smiling

when paying attention
to the smallest things
is everything

My Son

for Jesse Samuel Koch Statman

at thirteen
he's a young man
growing taller
it seems every day

one day he'll be taller
than me and then
he'll be taller
all the time

(A)political Poem

I think about politics all the time
but I don't write many
directly political poems.
Two things worry me:
the poem
grounded in a moment
becoming a week or month or year later
meaningless

the second thing
my fear
that writing the poem
I'll think somehow I've accomplished something
done what needs to be done
and can move on

One Person

dawn light and daylight
mixing in the clouds
I run for the subject
and there is none
red brick white brick
gray, dark windows,
I am breathing so hard
I have to stop
in the middle of the sidewalk
bent over
no one passing stops
to ask
no one even looks:
rooted, winded, I can't breathe
I am that alone
I want one person to care
one person who tonight
at dinner or
in front of the tv
or drinking in a bar
would remember

Late Afternoon

the rains have come
dumping enough water
to flood the streets
shimmering and slick
and at once I get the idea
how someone long ago
first conceived of Venice

in the green bowl on the table
three pieces of fruit:
a banana, two apples
they look old, brown splotches,
almost inedible
I throw them in the trash

the dog sighs, unconscious, in his sleep
cars roll hissing down the street
I notice that I'm frowning
but can't think of why

You and Me

I want to hold you hard
and I don't know how
I know you want me to
because you've said so
but if my hands don't
feel right to me
how could they feel right
to you?

Translating García Lorca

for Pablo Medina

the danger is not
that he'll take over
my poems
but that when it happens
I won't know

(image of cow, of horse
of cadaver or sleepy river
or a pure and less
than innocent love)

so when someone points it out
I won't see—
already eaten
devoured

Invisible Man

The moon is unambiguous
—John Ashbery

When all the stories are told
the stories of love and death
the stories of sadness and happiness
tragedy comedy
stories of a tree or a cup of coffee
sitting on a counter

There is a man talking with a woman
or a mother and child
while the father is thinking
I am the one left out
and he leaves
you can see his back
in the corner to the right
if you hold a magnifying glass to the old photo
that had been carried around in a wallet
and now sits on a desk
with other photos that look nothing like it
except they all display characters
from one life or another

When they are all told
I think—
having tried to make sense
having assembled them and wondered—
I figured out
that they're not conflicting stories
but rather stories that no one has attended to
(except those who told them
who were interested only

in their own versions)
and so had simply been ignored
(congenitally or cognitively)
or not heard at all

For example,
I told someone I thought
Ellison's *Invisible Man*
avoided the question of race
and he practically screamed at me that
race was everywhere
and I said yes, in our lives,
but not in the book
we were crossing the street at the yellow light
which meant everyone was supposed
to be ready to stop
were we daring when we kept on going
the moon is only really unambiguous to the moon
to the rest of the world
shouldn't there be other questions

A woman in Panama talking
to a woman in Geneva
is beautiful although
the woman in Geneva only thinks
of the beauty of her voice
and not the beauty of her Panamanian skin
or her black hair
or the way she is sitting with her ankles crossed
bare feet with painted pink toes
They have decided to speak in English
although the woman in Geneva thinks
her Spanish is probably better
but the woman in Panama wants
to speak in English
because she knows her accent

makes her sound almost British
The woman in Geneva asks
When your book is translated into German
will you ask a friend what it means
When translated into French
will you figure it out yourself

My friend looks at me
He says, so you think Ellison has it wrong
No, I said,
I just read a different book than you
It's like all these other books
and all these other stories
Like the Kennedy assassination story
there are so many versions
that the fact that he's dead
seems like an afterthought

After Kennedy was shot
I kept seeing him alive
I was in Kindergarten and
in all the films they showed us
he was there
smiling and waving
He was the President
And Lyndon Johnson was from Texas
where the President had been shot
I didn't know that then
I only knew that I'd been told
the President was dead
but there he was on the screen
in the classroom
where the teachers showed us the movie
even though they said
he wasn't President anymore

II. Yellow

Please Read This

that's how the page started
no salutation
no *dear* or *hello* or
I was thinking of you
just
please read this
but then there was no more
a blank paper page
that on a computer
would have been
an empty screen
a sky
would have been cloudless
at the movies
there'd have been no movie
how do you explain disappeared urgency
how do you explain
what doesn't follow
it seemed terrible
yet also to have been expected—
surf sounds, wind sounds,
what makes wordlessness so painful
and so normal
the word *please*
covers it all
we can explain the absent *this*
explain what can't be read
but not the *please*
we can explain
so much of *everything*
but not *please*
not here

Turbulence

if you fly
you know how to expect it
that it will be unexpected
it will be just the way the pilot turns
on the "Fasten Seat Belt Sign"
a set of symbols calling into question
the use of sign and symbols
though this seems unimportant
when you are cruising at an altitude
where the symbols and signs don't matter
nor does the flotation device
underneath your seat since the whole trip
is over dry land so what are you going
to do with that info now
you don't want this
in your life
you don't want a pilot or a sign
you want *her*
which is what you say
she says,
I really can't talk about this
you say,
we have to talk about this
she says,
that's your story
you say,
story story story
which is when she walks away
and you feel the sudden pull
of that seat belt
which is suddenly holding you back
which won't let you move

you know
it's a stupid metaphor
and you've been stupid
but here's unearned luck:
you haven't lost yet
you still have a chance
at a possible final future

Changing

the stores in
my neighborhood in Brooklyn
are always changing
a flower store
becomes a bookstore
a bookstore
becomes a cell phone store
a vacant lot a drug store
(when there are already at least
six or seven of those)
a grocery closes and becomes—
well, what
the sign says
commercial space available
when it used to say
family-owned since 1932
then a sign appears
and half of it will become a bank
but the other half is still unknown

the baseball season is over
it gets too hard
in September having to deal
with every game every day
the meaning of a win
or a loss
makes it hard to focus
on anything else
like the weather or the newspaper or cooking
in February that all changes
with pitchers and catchers reporting
dusting off winter

and starting spring
it's always this sudden wake-up
every year for me
they're playing baseball again
and there will be more new stores
in the neighborhood
new people on the block
looking out the window now
it's all gray
the beginning of a fall November rain
anticipating the heart of winter
one change after another
in the changelessness

A way to redeem the world

is not to fall in love
but to stay in love
to use the word love
every day in your life
and mean it
the way meaning
crowds out fear
and leaves room
for foolishness
for being wrong
a man on the street
sleeping in blankets and newspapers
dreams of hunger
a baby in a stroller cries
a girl on the subway
looks at her nails
which are long and colorful
her algebra book
in her lap
she thinks about how
she doesn't want
to go to school this day
but she knows she will
she knows she knows
how to answer even the questions
she'll never be asked
that's how hard she's studied
she smiles *because* she knows she knows
then she smiles again because this morning
her mother had made pancakes
she can lick her lips
and still taste the syrup

she loves her mother
suddenly, right now,
she even loves algebra
and the world
and there we are
a step closer to redemption
syrup, algebra, love

A Love Affair with Perception

you put yourself
in the movie
so you can feel
the wind and smell
the water
you ask the conductor
where the dining car is
you have pasta and wine
and back at your seat
you know you are
a little drunk

she is with you
in your arms
in the movie
and the world
she whispers
how much she loves you
it's a happy scene
which you suddenly realize
should be happening later
the words have started to change
there's a new screenwriter
you keep telling him
to leave it the way it is
you like it fine
but he smiles
he tells you he has a better idea
it will be more private, intimate
this worries you
how much at this point
should you reveal

how much should she know
would it give away
the ending
which *you* don't even know
you don't want to
being only in the middle
or at the beginning

Poem Written in Silence

for Colette Brooks

on the subway
a young black woman
writes in her notebook
dark eyes, thin dreads
pulled back over her head
next to her
a young white man reads zoology
and next to him
an older white man reads
the *Times*
he snaps the pages
frowning
the subway sometimes seems
the center of my life
like I've learned
everything I know on these trains
an Asian woman gets on
Delancey Street
her midriff showing bare
between white skirt and shirt
a Latino man reads *Diario*
starting at the sports
the way I do
I'm there
looking, watching, spying
on every conversation
in every different language:
English, Russian, Spanish, Greek
a couple sits across from me
wearing heavy overcoats
I try not to stare
as they sign every word
with their hands

You're in love

and your first thought
is what of it
it's happened before
and have the results
been all that great
she looks and sounds
like a variation
on a few of the other women
who have had
this effect on you
the cloud walk
sudden smile as
you remember why
you're having those feelings
you're feeling this good
the question is:
is it worth all this time
now she's holding your hand
and you're falling
into her eyes
falling
falling
falling
and the answer
yes, worth it, yes
even at the end
when it's over
and you're out the other side
and the world has gone rotten
it was worth it
just for when it happened
for the certainty
of how you'll feel
when it happens again

A Hundred

in the street a hundred women
I won't see again
—Paul Eluard

in the street
a hundred women
a hundred men
a hundred babies
a hundred trees
a hundred cars
that roll slowly by
their drivers not even
paying attention
to the rolling, to the drive
windows open
with music you don't
know if you know
because you only get
a few notes
a few words
about love or hurt
a *boom ta boom*
of rhythm
and then the car is gone

A Word Gone Wrong

those boys over in the park
are talking about
all the girls they'll pick up later
they punch one another
on the arm
they try cigarettes
and hide the coughing
one, smaller
maybe younger
wears a Bart Simpson T-shirt
and the others laugh
what girl would be seen with you

he walks off
picks up a rock
and throws it into the lake
he tries skipping others
but they just sink

he looks lost he defines alone
his friends start to leave
he shakes his head
he isn't going
they've laughed at him enough—
one boy says
they were just kidding
what they said
was just for fun
but he shakes his head at that
he says he doesn't care

Snow and ice

alone seem enough
as a title
to evoke
the image
of those different things
eventually packed
together

I have these ideas:
a country house
surrounded by snow
a frozen city
where no one walks outside
different silences
daytime, night

is it cold
how cold
so cold

a cold that
passes understanding

Meditation

I was walking
on 7th Avenue in Brooklyn
bright fall sky
bright afternoon
I passed
a young woman
wearing a black T-shirt
with white letters
they read:
Don't be a pussy
Eat one

The Happy Problem

he tried to explain to her
that being happy
was not the point
that happiness can happen
that those are moments
we should enjoy
especially because
as we get older
they seem relatively fewer
than when we were young
but there weren't really
more moments before
they just seemed that
much more intense
because we weren't used
to the experience
we can be as happy now
but the surprise
isn't there

she asked him if he was finished
he said *okay*
she said,
then what's the point
if being happy
is not the point
then what is?

look, he said,
I just don't like making
the complicated simple
she turned to him

but not so he saw her face
then why do you try
and explain everything
all the time
why do you think
that just because you say it
it's true?

a sadness suddenly filled him
because he knew she was right
that whatever he might have to say
went beyond any words he knew

Blindness

your world was once
more than sound

I want to defend you
but I don't know
from whom
or against what

the last thing
you think
you saw
was a coffeepot
on the counter
next to a mason jar with flowers
they were lilacs, you said,
lilacs and clematis
a lot of blue
and purple

I think how calm you are
when you remember

I think how I wish somehow
you could give that calm to me

The Bad Screenwriter

the details of your life
never concerned you
they were just there
because
that was what
life was made of
then the day came
when they weren't there
the screws had come loose and
some bad screenwriter had taken
over your life
and all you could do
was play the part

but the part was all wrong
it wasn't who you'd been
ever wanted to be
it was crazy
you were crazy
you wanted to tell
the writer to stop
but this was his story
and not yours
though he made it *feel*
like yours and
all you could do was go along
with words you didn't know
with feelings you didn't
know you had
you weren't even able to wonder
how long will this last
because it wasn't in the plot yet

or if it was
you didn't know

only the screenwriter knew
and he was evil

People Shouting

Usually, it's to make a point like
"Watch out for that car!"
Or
"No! No!"
so the baby won't put its fingers
into the socket.

But some people shout
as a way to say hello
or a way to tell their stories.
They don't listen for
a response and too often
there's none anyway.

It's not a need to be heard:
It's a kind of loneliness.
They just want to speak,
to put a story into the world:
All their hopes right there.

A Poem about Something Ending Is an Elegy

for Elaine Savory

rain turned to snow
overnight
a whole city covered

though already we're halfway into spring
new green finally almost here
but some trees still with no leaves
the buds sit hard
but now the snow
the cold
some early pink and white blossoms
have fallen
they're in the snow
scattered
so many blossoms
after battle

this isn't a sad poem though
it's a poem of spring and
winter facts

Subway Manners

for Sam Scherer

I.

a green sweater
a silver necklace
herself in the window glass
she realized
she had missed the express
but the local would be okay
the man with the glasses looked at her
then looked away
she pretended it hadn't happened
his look had seemed so long on longing
she could always come back to him
she could always slide over
and let him know
she was sorry for their lost, failed love
he got off at the next stop

II.

newspaper under his arm
her grandfather had taught her
that when you were done with your paper
you should turn and offer it
to the person next to you
just as you got off the train
the man's paper had had
American flags on it
the late city final

of a late city day
the late city final
had been her grandfather's paper
her grandmother always complained
how he never brought it home
his city wasn't her grandmother's
it was hers
city of trains and newspapers
of voices she listened to in secret
faces she looked at once
and not again

Snow, Late March, Brooklyn

here it comes
sideways with the wind
racing down this street
and everything is dusted by it
cars, trees, ground
but it's the end of March
for God's sake
spring is *here*
so of course it melts
and it keeps that up
snowing and melting
all afternoon
and everyone
and by this I mean *everyone*
even the little kids who in November
would have been oohing
dreams of sledding and snowmen
just wish it would stop
and finally leave us alone

this was one long winter
it was cold and snowy
and it's time for it to be over
we have bats and gloves
in the hallway
waiting for their turn
let winter come
at its time again
but for now, *for right now,*
let us move on

Love in the Time of Cholera

you cried
at the place in the novel
where her husband died

she sits in a room
full of their books and their furniture
paintings, emptiness, dust
just before the time
when she has
the rest of her life to live
just before
she realizes
she won't know
what that will be

you thought reflexively
how you are not her
you aren't a fiction
you aren't created
but you wondered
why you were crying

the book had a yellow cover
the sun made
a yellow softness on the floor
the word yellow repeated in your head
over and over
yellow yellow, yellow yellow

he was dead that page
she is alive the next

you turned pages read pages
turned pages read pages
the whole afternoon until
it was an evening sun
then the sun set
and all the yellow was gone

III. Tourist at a Miracle

Tourist

hubo un milagro, she said,
a miracle
but in such a quiet voice
I had to ask her
to say it again
which she did
she didn't like it like that
a voces (loud)
it didn't seem as true anymore
she looked at me
it seemed just then
she must hate me
must hate anyone like me
she pointed down the road
curving, dusty
she said it was the way to the ruins
I didn't know
if I wanted to go
I already knew
I wouldn't see what she had seen

More the Imagined than the Real

I'm always caught
in that problem
of how what I hope for
is
more the imagined than the real
not that what we see
isn't spectacular
mountains, river, lakes
bright lights, neon, and crowds
people whose eyes keep looking
for what's there and far beyond
maybe it just all gets better
the second time around
you know
where you're going
what isn't worth
returning to
I've always loved surprise
but *Anna Karenina* was better
the second time
and even more troubling the third
Yes Anna and Don't Anna
and what is Levin talking about
a small boy waits for his mother
for birthday after birthday
until he's a man
older he wonders how to prevent
confusion
to prevent remembered love
from turning into hatred
when memory of his mother
comes to mind

the car turns off the highway
this stop has a girl
behind a counter
selling burgers, hot dogs, pizza
she reads a book
while waiting
she looks up
takes orders
serves food
then hands out change

she says thank you
when we put a tip in the jar
the red and green mountains
rise up behind her
the couple next to us
fusses with the smiling baby
in its stroller
the father takes a photo
mountain desert backdrop
with a mother and her child

Fields

of butterflies

Golden Sulphur, Painted Lady
Monarch, Sandhill Skipper—

so many as though
they'd replaced the grass

Kim said
she'd never seen
such multitudes flying up

as she walked

the air filled
with endless colored wings

This Belongs To

the tree frog sound today
sounds the same as
last night's cricket
though I'm sure this isn't true
cricket tree frog same
still my ears hear
what my ears hear
I am not confused
by crow call and blue-jay caw
I can tell the difference
between passenger train rattle
and freight
though if asked
to describe
I'd have no good response
beyond the shoulder shrug of
"oh, you know..."
a dog barks
dogs bark more
sound of pick-up on a half-paved road
bee drone
fly buzz
from the radio float
spring training baseball voices
I turn the sound off
and the game isn't there
the rest of the afternoon

Tubing

for Luisa Giugliano

As we started my son
Jesse talked about technology
how the people who invent things
never know all the things
their inventions will eventually do.

After one small stretch of rapids
into a longer stretch of calm
we shifted to what was there:

the sky, dazzling
the river, cool
a blue heron sailing high
purple and blue dragonflies coupling
flowers emerging from the rock
and trees and green all along
the river's side:
Queen Anne's Lace
Joe Pye weed
and something
whose name I couldn't remember.

Yellow Jerusalem artichoke
Jesse said, telling me
how a friend of a friend's father
had started a company
that made pasta out of the roots.

Fly Fishing

I didn't know all the rules
I was breaking and inventing
as love, turning into a river,
turned away
and left the countryside
for the more familiar city.

Did I write love
I meant silence
and music:
So I left, returned
unbridled, rose
smiled, turned, clipped, shook
withdrew, mistook
misstepped, undid.

But I had something,

a smallmouth bass
or a rainbow trout
the river early spring freezing
fingers numb
legs, feelings numb.

This became an unexpected education.
Watch yourself, I heard myself think.
Always watch yourself.

Late Night

for Jane LeCroy

he accidentally spilled
some water on the floor
an accident is an accident
he thought
even in places like this
near the desert
so it didn't really matter
a spill
but the lake is lower
than anyone can remember
the constant prediction of rain
is none
and never
the moon tonight is full
with its own silver haze
he thought about Orion
and Orion's Belt
which he thought he recognized
because once someone had pointed it out
Orion's Belt, look, there
he towels up the water
hangs the towel
on a hook
he'd told her
loneliness was not his problem
but being alone
was something else
he didn't need to remember her face
it was passive and lost in thought

a few feet away
it was that moon
it was her face
it was Orion/Orion's Belt
the slow listless drama
of spilling water

Tú Quieres Saber

de pronto entiendo es una pregunta
y yo contesto nada
as in
suddenly I understand it is a question
and I answer nothing
the days are too streaky
running into each other
without good reasons
which is why memory always seems
so relevant and present
no difference between
a short time ago and
a long time ago
when I use one phrase
say, are we there?
I might as well have used the other
where are we?
even though
this seems to confuse
anyone I talk to
then I'm confused too
weren't we just in Mexico
or Costa Rica
or Nicaragua
Colombia? Ecuador? Peru
didn't we just drive to Nova Scotia
didn't we talk
aren't you dead
and you
and you
can I have another drink
aren't I already drinking

así es: so it is
una cabeza llena de preguntas
a head full of questions
a month full of questions
hello, this is September
sometimes for thirty days
sometimes forever

The Poetry City Hall of Fame

when the executive committee met
for the first time
everyone knew there'd be trouble
so they decided
on only one requirement:
if you want to be in
you're in

and has *that* been a success
no one wanted to be
the first
to appear to *want* to be there
so the place is empty
the building just sits there
an architectural success of
Greek and modern styles
it has a beautiful rose garden
benches, shade trees,
visitors come and sit here
for hours and hours
some reading, some writing
not a lot of talking
some seem happy to do
nothing at all

A Thousand Words

I.

sliver twilight moon
a thousand words:
navigator, Laundromat, oak
orange construction cones
this evening
the park is full of snow and trees
someone asked will you bring me
a meteorite stone from Las Vegas?
I said,
but I'm not going to Las Vegas
and she answered
but if you do
you can find them everywhere

II.

in this twilight
I can barely find the moon
directly under it in the sky
is Venus, the evening star
that's no star at all
the wind comes fiercely out of the bushes
and I fall, knocked over, into snow
a thousand more words in my head:
beach, locked, canvas,
pencil, bench, pine
a thousand words:
heights, lost, heights
resolve, view, found
it gets darker

and the sliver moon brighter
I see the vaguer outline
of the shadowed moon's circle
too many stars now
to see Venus
now I'm surprised
because there's a shooting star
a comet, a meteor
what are the other names for it

III.

months later
I arrived in Las Vegas
to be in the orange and fire desert and not
the orange and neon strip
the meteorite rocks
crumbled in my hands
each time I picked one up
it fell away
on my dresser at home
is a piece of volcanic rock
solid, volcanic brown
but, she said,
you're not supposed to
take rocks from the volcano
it brings bad luck when you do
it's from Vesuvius, I answer
and there I am in Brooklyn
all the same, she said, all the same
she was thinking of the ruined Italian city
you should put it back, she said,
when you can

Neutral Location

what you
make this
city you
make half
in love
half in
despair
its music
is beating
out windows
out doors
its trucks
its trains
its cars
from bridge
to bridge
from street
to street
from one
more body
we take
up space
that isn't
really there
that really
hasn't been
for ages
our time
tom toms
and streaks
by it
shakes, thunders

glistens, parades
you wonder
what the
city you've
made is
made of
language you
think maybe
that nothing
more you
wonder how
to explain
to someone
far away
how to
get there

Because I Live in This City

for Mark Larrimore

because I live in this city
I feel I hardly know it

there are landmarks
and parks
questions and languages
I float by
always on my way
point to point
calculating shortest distances
fastest trips
easiest way to get
to where I know I want and need to be

I think I would like to be
more of a tourist
in the city
more of a tourist
in my life
paying attention and
getting excited
I want to gawk a little more

She Wanted to Be Looked At

you name it, he said
as the train left West 4th to go uptown
they've got everything you want
juice, coffee, all that stuff
you like for breakfast
she listened and leaned
on his shoulder
deep breath, her eyes closed
I warned you, he said,
I told you you weren't
going to sleep enough
you stay up all night with the tv
all your parties
she didn't want to answer
she turned to her sister
sitting next to her
her other side
you know, she said
you shouldn't dress like that
sister still in last night's clothes
both were still in last night's clothes
your tits are *flying* out
men walked by
their eyes dragged to her chest
the sister looked back at her sister
who was leaning against her boyfriend
thought how it was easy for her sister to talk
when *she* already had
someone to lean on
you'll be there, he said,
after that night last night
your music and your drinking and your drugs

but you won't remember a damned thing
your brain just melts
she closed her eyes again
so that's what it was
her brain was melting
her sister's breasts
floated in front of her closed eyes
we've got to take the bus cross town
he said, it's too far for me to walk

Music Central

for Jennifer Wilson

on this one F train
on violin and trombone
two men are playing
"Those Were the Days"
a song from when
I was young
about a woman growing older
I remember watching
the singer sing it
on television
I think, was it the *Ed Sullivan Show*
now someone is
playing an accordion
something sweet
and just as familiar
though I can't put
a name to it
at the next stop
Second Avenue
he's off the train
but like
"Those Were the Days"
it's a song from when
I was young
when really there weren't any days
to remember or regret
the way there are now

WTC (July 2006)

the towers were ugly
I couldn't stand
how they changed the skyline
but they've been
a part of me
more than just because
the city's where I live
my grandfather worked on them
not in, *on*
a master electrician
the wiring and circuits
lights and power
were *his*
he was proud of what he'd done
we went to the opening
not the public one
the one for all the people
who'd made the towers happen
we couldn't wait
my older brother Dave, me
they were giving out
blue construction hard hats to all the kids
only they ran out before our turn
the organizers surprised
by how many people
we rode the elevators up and down
my grandfather, Sam,
who my son Jesse Samuel
is named for
smiled
we looked at the city
the water, sky

I never went again
but I still have this empty feeling
these years later
staring south down 6th Avenue
from 11th Street where I teach
they aren't there
the city's towers, my grandfather's towers
their absence so obvious
I can't believe
what I'm not seeing

City Summers

are not
my favorite
everywhere too
tired, humid
wrong smells
midday rot
as you
walk by
certain restaurants
stores where
garbage spills
a thickening
liquid runs
out from
sidewalk to
street where
even cleaned
by the
biggest summer
thunderstorm it
needs only
a few
hours to
grow to
rot again

all year
I think
longingly of
summer and
here it
is mid-July

I want
to close
the windows
turn on
the a.c.
lights off
away from
heat away
from smells
next winter
ice and
cold and
snow already
coming next
winter already
arriving in
my head

Travel

sometimes it becomes elusive:
a half inch as one hundred miles
will not be the same
depending on the road you're on
the thick blue of the interstate versus
this red line
which means you'll wind back and forth
and the speed limit
will slow you down
with Slow Down signs
and traffic lights
as you go through one small town
after another
with getting anywhere
eventually somehow ceasing
to be the point

at a small roadside shop
you buy a clear glass vase
on which someone has painted
light blue ribbons
you buy a book
The Audubon Society Pocket Guides
Familiar Birds of North America
Eastern Region
with the Blue Jay (*Cyanocitta cristata*)
on the cover
because even if you can't
recognize the birds in the distance
you want to know their names,
not the ones you already know:
        Red-winged Blackbird (*Agelaius phoeniceus*)

Ring-necked Pheasant (*Phasianus colchicus*)
Herring Gull (*Larus argentatus*)
but the ones you don't
Rose-breasted Grosbeak (*Pheucticus ludovicanus*)
Greater Scaup (*Aythya marila*)
Common Goldeneye (*Bucephala clangula*)
they make all kinds of sounds
are found in woods or near water
are invisible from here
in the car
the car on the red line road

you stop for the night
small inn, sunset deck
did you hear that
it was the stopped car cooling down
it was the tissue paper wrapped around
the morning-glory-painted vase
it was the *chewy-chewy-chewy chew chew chew*
of the American Redstart (*Setophaga ruticilla*)
that dropped from the trees
down to the grass
and seemed first to look at you
then through you
it had no sense of time passing
and for a minute or a moment
neither did you

Acknowledgments

Some of these poems have appeared in *Hanging Loose, The Cincinnati Review*, *Trespass*, *The Hat*, *The Duplications*, *Infinity (and Other Inventions)*, and *Ping Pong*.

I want to thank the Virginia Center for the Creative Arts for its support of my work in 2007, 2008 and 2009. In addition, I want to acknowledge the support of my friends and colleagues, my students, and the administration at Eugene Lang College, The New School for the Liberal Arts.

This manuscript has been many years in the making and many readers have advised me and consoled me. I want to thank my mentor, father-in-law and impossible and wonderful friend, the late Kenneth Koch, as well as Jordan Davis, Mary Crowley, and Ben Kligler for looking at early drafts of something called *Poetry City* and their thoughtful and valuable advice. I want to thank Pablo Medina, my collaborator on *Poeta en Nueva York*, and *mi hermano en poesía* for reading *Poetry City* and the manuscript *Celia Cruz fue la voz and Other Poems* for the same and for being so tough on me. I thank my son Jesse, who has been an astute critic for a long time, an appreciative reader beyond his years. There aren't really words for what Katherine means to the poems, so I won't even try. Thanks to the folks at Hanging Loose for this, in particular to Dick Lourie for his acute and clear copy-editing on the manuscript, but mostly to Donna Brook, who took three (the third, an unformed something or other called *Invisible Man*) manuscripts and found something whole and distinct inside them. As an editor, she is a gift. Even more, because of Donna, the world is a better place.